Diana

Diana

The People's Princess

Melissa Burdick Harmon

MetroBooks

MetroBooks

An Imprint of the Michael Friedman Publishing Group, Inc.

Library of Congress Cataloging-in-Publication Data

Harmon, Melissa Burdick.
    Diana : the people's princess / Melissa Burdick Harmon
        p. cm.
    Includes bibliographical references (p.) and index.
    ISBN 1-58663-581-6 (alk. paper)
        1. Diana, Princess of Wales, 1961---Pictorial works. 2. Princesses--
Great Britain--Biography--Pictorial works. I. Title.

    DA591.A45 D531726 2003
    941.085'092--dc21
    [B]
                                                            200206771

Art Director: Kevin Ullrich
Designer: Midori Nakamura
Photography Editor: Paquita Bass
Production Director: Richela Fabian Morgan

Color separations by Radstock Repro
Printed in England by Butler & Tanner

1 3 5 7 9 10 8 6 4 2

For bulk purchases and special sales, please contact:
Michael Friedman Publishing Group, Inc.
Attention: Sales Department
230 Fifth Avenue
New York, NY 10001
212/685-6610 FAX 212/685-3916

Visit our website:
www.metrobooks.com

Contents

 bove: Princess Diana won the hearts of millions with her unaffected manner, her tremendous capacity for compassion, and her ability to relate to people from all walks of life.

Introduction

*S*he took us by surprise.

From the moment that news of Lady Diana Spencer's relationship with Prince Charles broke, the tall, shy teenager with the big eyes and blushing English rose complexion came to dominate front pages around the world. She smiled from hundreds of magazine covers. She appeared—at first looking timid and awkward, but quickly gaining self-possession—on the nightly news. She became ubiquitous, a part of our everyday lives.

That's because the press, quite simply, fell head over heels in love with her. And that was one relationship in her short life that would last. Over the course of seventeen years, reporters everywhere covered everything about the multifaceted woman we came to call simply "Diana."

Much of the world fell in love with her, too. But for us, it wasn't because she was good fodder for photographs and articles. For us, it was that she seemed to offer—we hoped against hope—living proof that stories like *Cinderella* and *Snow White* can come true.

After all, Lady Diana Spencer was earning her living cleaning other people's houses and tending other people's children when she began to interest Prince Charles. Could she actually capture and keep the heart of the heir to the throne of the United Kingdom? Oh how we hoped she could.

Not, of course, because we cared all that much about whom Prince Charles married. Neither the press nor the public had ever found Charles, eldest son of the long-reigning

Queen Elizabeth II, all that scintillating. We cared because we wanted the shy, unpretentious girl—who from the very beginning showed a remarkable ability to empathize with people—to become princess, just like those other fairy-tale girls we'd been hearing about since we were two years old.

But of course those classic stories of happily ever after end with the words "I do." They never reveal what happens after the blissful couple runs down the church steps. And it is after this point that Diana's own personal story often becomes dark, indeed.

bove: The Prince and Princess of Wales—looking like they stepped out of the pages of a storybook—caused a worldwide upswing of interest in the British royal family, with Diana being given the treatment generally reserved for superstars.

For a while, though, Diana and Charles did give us the spun-sugar version of the fairy tale. We watched the two fall in love, not knowing that Diana had been required to call her boyfriend "Sir" until after the engagement was formally announced. We were caught up in the heady days of the engagement itself, not realizing that the teenage princess-to-be was so lonely that she had taken to spending time in the servants' area at Buckingham Palace—only to be thrown out by the Yeoman of the Glass and China. And we were unaware that she was suffering from the damaging cycle of bulimia, forcing herself to lose lots of weight very quickly before her wedding.

Oblivious to Diana's personal troubles, we eagerly turned on our television sets, even as 750 million other people did the same, to see the wedding, the dress, the guests. We were thrilled when, just two months later, Diana became pregnant. We were proud of her swift evolution, becoming poised royalty, then beloved celebrity, almost without missing a beat—and all the while combating morning sickness.

Diana was still only twenty years old when she proudly presented to the world the new heir to the crown, Prince William—blonde and adorable, looking just like her. Just two years later, she once again stood on the hospital steps, this time delightedly displaying the "spare," Prince Harry, who would take the throne should anything happen to William. This time, however, she often appeared alone in photographs with the new baby.

But we still thought we were reading about Cinderella. We didn't yet know that she was fighting desperate emotional demons and frantically trying to protect a crumbling marriage. We just knew that we saw something vulnerable about her. Surely anyone who could so easily tune into the troubles of others had to have problems of her own.

Indeed, Diana's ability to connect with those who were suffering contributed tremendously to her universal appeal. She played many different roles during her years as Princess of Wales. But it was her work with dozens and dozens of charities—and her one-on-one relationships with the people served by those charities—that led her to achieve the goal she expressed in the infamous BBC interview that helped precipitate her divorce. Suspecting at that point that she would never become Queen of England, she said she wanted instead to become a "queen of people's hearts."

Over the years, Diana helped to raise not only many millions for her charities, but also public awareness. She was talking about AIDS—and embracing dying AIDS patients in front of the cameras—when much of the planet was just coming to terms with the disease. She reminded the world that leprosy is not some remote illness relegated to biblical times, but still a real threat in many Third World nations. Later in her life, she even took on the politically charged issue of land mines, creating a profound and lasting concern for the issue. She also reminded us that battered women and children right in our backyards are just as much in need of our concern as are people dying in distant lands.

Left: Diana converses with a child—dressed to the nines for her big moment—at the official opening of the Broadwater Nursery Unit in South London.

We also heard Diana confess her own private battles against the dark worlds of eating disorders and despair. By sharing her problems with the public, Diana let us know that we're not alone in facing down illness and sorrow. Maybe she wasn't the *perfect* princess any longer—Cinderella never talked of suicide, after all—but she was *our* princess. Moreover, she was someone who had troubles just like we do, and she didn't pretend otherwise.

Even as she was turning what might have been routine royal charity work into something much more, however, she was also developing in other, very different, areas of her life. Recognizing—and respecting—the importance of the millions of people who adored her from afar, Diana always took care to look like someone worthy of the spotlight. She regularly cautioned her hairdresser to do his absolute best, because the people waiting to see her expected it. She knew that looking fabulous was part of her job. And in doing so, she became the most photographed woman in history.

Along the way, she developed a real fashion consciousness. Prior to Diana's entrance into the family, the words "pizzazz" and "House of Windsor" were hardly synonymous. She proved that it *is* possible to wear a hat and carry a purse—key elements in the Windsor look—and still knock 'em dead. Later, she started to have fun with fashion, donning everything from red polka-dot ankle socks to off-the-shoulder cocktail dresses revealing every inch of her hourglass figure. She became nothing less than a fashion icon.

Neither ambassador to the world nor fashion icon was at the top of Diana's list of priorities, though. That top spot was held by quite a different position: the role of Mummy. Diana made a huge effort to raise her two boys to become humane young men—gracious human beings as well as effective princes.

Indeed, Diana saw William and Harry through many difficult times: through a foundering marriage, a heartbreaking separation, and divorce. She also helped the boys handle the difficulties they encountered attending private schools with ordinary children (always under the watchful eye of a policeman), as well as deal with the press's endless scrutiny. Ultimately, she left them with the courage and strength to survive the greatest trial of all, her own death at the young age of thirty-six.

Shortly before her brief life came to an end, Diana gave an interview to the French magazine *Le Monde*, in which she said, "I am much closer to people at the bottom than to people at the top." It was true. It is ultimately why she took our hearts.

It is also why, at the end of the day, she had become the most beloved member of the royal family. It is why we followed her life with such interest. And when she later became a figure of terrible tragedy, it is why we wept for her. And missed her. And mourned her.

Right: Diana comforts Prince William after he has had a hard time at his school's Sports Day.

PART ONE

Growing Up

The beautiful teenager, her face still showing the last traces of baby fat, smiles shyly at the camera. She wears a bright blue suit—carefully chosen with her mother's help—purchased off-the-rack at Harrods. She also sports a mammoth ring, a large sapphire circled with diamonds, the gems paid for by her future mother-in-law. The older man—he is thirty-two, she a mere nineteen—stands behind her, on a higher step so that he can tower over her, despite her 5'10" (1.8m) height. He, too, looks genuinely happy as he faces the camera.

Huge crowds gathered in front of Buckingham Palace on that historic Tuesday morning, February 24, 1981, since former prime minister Edward Heath had leaked news of the forthcoming announcement to London's *Times*. In the midst of the chaos, the young girl's father happily roamed among the gathered press and public, snapping photos of his child. His third daughter—the one born only because he and his wife were trying so desperately for a male heir—was about to announce her engagement. And what an engagement it was.

Cameras whirred and pencils flew as the press captured the official announcement that Charles, Prince of Wales and heir to the throne of the United Kingdom, and Lady Diana Spencer, daughter of one of England's oldest and most aristocratic families, intended to marry. It looked like the perfect fairy-tale ending to a modern-day Cinderella story. And if some people in the crowd were doubtful as to whether the Prince of Wales was really in love with his future princess, there was no doubt in anyone's mind that the press and public adored her.

Above: When thirty-two-year-old Prince Charles asked nineteen-year-old Lady Diana Spencer if she would like to marry him, she modestly replied, "Yes, please." The couple officially announced their engagement on February 24, 1981, at Buckingham Palace. Upon seeing the engagement photos, Diana decided to go on a diet immediately. Unfortunately, this course of action resulted in bulimia and a dramatic loss of weight.

Lady Diana Spencer, the media's valentine, was born on July 1, 1961, in her parents' bedroom at Park House on the royal estate of Sandringham. Her proud father, Edward John "Johnnie" Spencer, then Viscount Althorp and heir to the seventh Earl Spencer, noted at the time that little Diana Frances was "a superb physical specimen." What he did not say publicly was that she was also a specimen of the wrong sex. For Johnnie Spencer and his wife Frances, twelve years his junior, were desperate for a son.

The couple already had two daughters: Sarah, born in 1955, and Jane, born in 1957. In 1960, Frances Spencer had given birth to a much-longed-for son, but the child, named John, lived only ten hours. The next try resulted in Diana, a thoroughly unnecessary child in the great scheme of titles and inheritances. And of that, Diana was keenly aware. (In fact, she would tell people that she was supposed to be a boy.) Thankfully the necessary male child, Charles, who is now the ninth Earl Spencer, arrived three years later.

Young Diana grew up something of a loner, partly because her sisters were so much older. She often played by herself in her nursery; in later years, she stated that she didn't feel connected to anyone.

Nonetheless, the large ten-bedroom house was a great place to explore and play. There were all kinds of pets, there was a swimming pool, and the Spencer children were completely exempt from performing household tasks. Diana would roar down the driveway aboard her bright blue tricycle and receive a new doll for every birthday. When younger brother Charles arrived on the scene, she turned him into a bit of a plaything. The royal family would sometimes vacation at Sandringham, so Diana got to know them quite well. Once, at the age of five, she was found in the midst of a heated game of hide-and-seek with Prince Andrew and Queen Elizabeth II.

It may have been one of Diana's last carefree moments, as the following year, Frances Spencer, having accomplished her duty of producing a male heir, and also having fallen wildly in love with the wealthy and charming Peter Shand Kydd, left home. At first, she took Diana and Charles to London with her, but upon returning to Park House with them at Christmas, she was given notice that the children would not be accompanying her back to London. A fierce two-year-long custody battle ensued. Johnnie Spencer won the children, but had little idea of what to do with them. He would join them for long, uncomfortable teas, during which he apparently struggled to think of things to say.

Diana was traumatized by her parents' divorce. In one instance, when each parent presented her with a dress to wear to a cousin's wedding, she fretted endlessly over which to choose, horrified by the thought of appearing to favor either loved one. She was, in fact, so upset by the marital breakup that she proclaimed she would never marry unless she truly loved the man, as she never wanted to be divorced.

School proved to be challenging for Diana, perhaps because she was in a state of emotional upheaval. First, she spent two years at Silfield, a nearby day school, where she cherished

Above: A loving family portrait of the Spencers, missing only a mother. Diana (far right) always idolized her eldest sister, Sarah (far left). Charles, the long-awaited heir, sits next to his father, who frequently failed to relate to the children he had fought so hard to keep. Jane (second from right) was always the most serious of the sisters.

the fairy tale–like stories of the kings and queens of England she heard. She showed signs of artistic talent, carefully dedicating every picture to "Mummy and Daddy," despite the fact that her parents were barely speaking. Diana won an award for trying hard.

At age nine, Diana was sent to Riddlesworth Hall, a preparatory school where she won a series of diving cups. She also received a prize for "Best-Kept Pet," her treasured guinea pig Peanuts, who was a key source of affection during those difficult years. She enjoyed studying dance and piano, but was less enthusiastic about academics. "I'm as thick as two short planks," she would often say, even as an adult, to the delight of the crowds who appreciated her humility. Her classmates called her "Thicky Spencer."

Diana then moved on to West Heath, an exclusive boarding school in Kent. She did not excel there either. A dreamer and a romantic, she would spend long hours lost in Barbara Cartland novels, where the virginal young lady always wins the titled gentleman. She longed to become a dancer, often sneaking downstairs in the night to practice. She remained somewhat immature for her age, and a little bit pudgy. And she twice failed every one of her O-level exams, which must be passed before students can begin to prepare for university admission.

In 1975, Diana's grandfather died, making her father the eighth Earl Spencer. The family moved to the vast estate at Althorp—a cold, museumlike mansion that had been home to fifteen generations of Spencers.

Soon after, the big-haired, ruffled-and-rhinestoned, outspoken Raine, Countess of Dartmouth—and daughter of romance novelist Barbara Cartland—appeared on the scene. Tenacious, she refused to be deterred by the Spencer children's nickname for her ("Acid Raine") or by the choruses of "Raine, Raine go away" that they would chant. Simply put, the children loathed her. Diana even had a friend write her a poison-pen letter.

On July 14, 1976, well aware of his children's feelings and without telling them of his plans, Johnnie Spencer married Raine in a brief civil ceremony. Fifteen-year-old Diana didn't know whether to be furious or heartbroken. Two years later, the fifty-four-year-old Earl Spencer suffered a severe stroke. He recovered, but was unable to speak for several months. He was never the same. Diana and her siblings felt that Raine kept them away from their father's bedside during this terrible time.

Meanwhile, Diana achieved her longtime dream of moving to London. There, she did housecleaning through an agency called "Solve Your Problems," babysat, and helped cater parties. Leisure time was devoted to watching soap operas with her roommates, dining on shepherd's pie and bacon sandwiches, learning to drive, and playing practical jokes on friends. Later, she became a teacher's helper at Young England School in Pimlico, where she taught the kindergarten children to draw, read to them, and showed them simple dance steps.

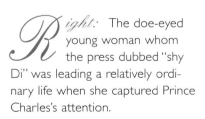

Right: The doe-eyed young woman whom the press dubbed "shy Di" was leading a relatively ordinary life when she captured Prince Charles's attention.

By this time, Lady Diana Spencer was on the brink of becoming a real beauty; but she wasn't terribly accomplished and she certainly wasn't leading a regal lifestyle. It is somewhat surprising, then, that she managed to catch the eye of the man who would be king.

Prince Charles had dated Diana's sister Sarah and knew Diana through her. He liked Diana's freshness, her ability to laugh, and the fact that she didn't seem intimidated by him. He began inviting this most aristocratic of cleaning ladies to house parties and other grand get-togethers. This was followed by a series of "cozy" suppers in his rooms at Buckingham Palace. He took her to see Highgrove, the eighteenth-century home he had bought in Gloucestershire, and asked her if she would help him decorate it. The press was beside itself with joy. Diana was charming, photogenic, and friendly. The press was determined that she marry Charles. So was the Queen Mother. So, perhaps, were Queen Elizabeth II and Prince Philip.

Early in 1981, Charles proposed to his teenage girlfriend, who had never had a boyfriend—virtually never had a date—before she began seeing him. Delirious with joy, Diana accepted, saying, "Yes, please," and adding "I love you so much, I love you so much."

Cinderella, the unhappy little girl who cleaned houses and tended children for a living, had captured the prince.

Right: People turned out in droves whenever the future Princess of Wales would appear in public, as at this event in Tetbury, Gloucestershire. They loved her for her openness, common touch, and vulnerability. And, of course, they loved her for her seemingly fairy-tale life.

Left: Diana Frances Spencer was born on July 1, 1961, at Park House, a ten-bedroom Victorian home on the royal estate of Sandringham in Norfolk, England. Her aristocratic parents, Johnnie Spencer, then Viscount Althorp, and Frances Spencer (née Roche) had been eager for a male heir, causing Diana—their third daughter—to view herself as a disappointment.

Right: Diana claimed that her earliest memory was the smell of the inside of her pram. Relatively shy, the young girl often played alone in her nursery. It was there that a sixteen-year-old Prince Charles unwittingly first caught sight of his future wife, who was only three years of age at the time.

Left: Diana, at age six, looks after her younger brother, Charles Spencer. Sadly, their mother had left home to be with the wealthy Peter Shand Kydd. Diana would often hear young Charles crying in the night; she longed to comfort him but was paralyzed by her fear of the dark.

Right: Diana is pictured here at age nine on summer holiday in West Sussex, not long before heading off to the loneliness of boarding school. During that year, she spent far more time with her pet guinea pig, Peanuts, than with either of her parents.

Above: Diana (sixth from left in second row from top) poses with classmates at Riddlesworth Hall in Diss, Norfolk. The desperately homesick child excelled at diving, dancing, and piano playing, but did poorly in academic subjects. Fellow students took to calling her "Thicky Spencer."

Left: At age twelve, Diana was sent to a new school, West Heath, near Sevenoaks, Kent. While her older sisters, Sarah and Jane, had performed well there, Diana did not follow in their footsteps. Instead, she buried herself in Barbara Cartland's romance novels, followed the life of Prince Charles (then dating her sister Sarah), and dreamed of becoming a professional dancer, often rising in the middle of the night to practice.

Right: By 1974, Diana was becoming a beauty, as shown in this photograph taken during a visit with her mother in Scotland's Outer Hebrides. Diana's relationship with Frances Shand Kydd would always be strained. In 1976, her father (who had become Earl Spencer by this point) married Raine, Countess of Dartmouth, without telling his children of his plans to do so. The four Spencer siblings called their new stepmother "Acid Raine."

Below: Sixteen-year-old Diana served as a bridesmaid at the marriage of her twenty-one-year-old sister Jane to thirty-five-year-old Robert Fellowes, Queen Elizabeth's Assistant Private Secretary. In the years that followed, Diana would often turn to Jane for advice; however, the siblings' relationship became strained when Fellowes, who was promoted to Private Secretary to the Queen—a position he still holds—appeared to be working against Diana.

Above: After failing all of her O-level exams and undergoing a brief stint at a Swiss finishing school, Diana—who had been longing to go to London—moved into her mother's Cadogan Square apartment. During this time, she remained romantically unattached, believing that boyfriends were nothing but trouble. Her sister Sarah, meanwhile, dated Prince Charles briefly before moving on to marry a relative of the loathed stepmother, Raine. Both siblings received invitations to Prince Charles's thirtieth birthday party.

Left: A coming-of-age gift from her parents and a generous bequest from her American great-grandmother enabled Diana to buy her own flat at 60 Coleherne Court, where, she later recalled, she spent the happiest days of her life.

Right: In July 1980, Diana received an invitation to spend a weekend at Petworth House in West Sussex, where the events included watching Prince Charles play polo at nearby Cowdray Park. At the barbecue that followed, Diana and Charles sat together on a bale of hay and had their first serious conversation. After this instance, they began to see each other with greater frequency.

Below: Diana suddenly found herself spending a great deal of time watching polo, the game being such a key part of Prince Charles's life. Here, her companion is Charles's good friend Camilla Parker-Bowles. Diana was surprised at how often Camilla would be included in their social activities, and by how much Camilla seemed to know about Charles. Still naive, however, Diana remained unaware of the fact that the prince and the married Camilla were involved in a longstanding relationship.

Left: The press immediately became enchanted by the photogenic girl they called "shy Di," relentlessly pursuing her all around London. Eager to please, she agreed to pose for pictures at the kindergarten where she was working, not realizing that her skirt was transparent. Horrified by the published images, she wept about the incident in private; however, she assured the members of the press that she knew they were just doing their job.

Below: Only a few days after the formal announcement of her engagement to Prince Charles, Diana is working hard for "the Firm," as the royal family refers to itself. During a visit to Cheltenham, Gloucestershire, she charms schoolboy Nicholas Hardy, who kisses her hand after presenting her with a daffodil. Diana would make thousands of such appearances during her royal tenure.

Above: Diana made a serious misstep at her first formal function after the engagement by donning black, which the royal family wears only for mourning. Moreover, the dress featured a dangerously revealing décolletage. Charles was livid when he saw the daring outfit, which Diana—showing some mettle—refused to change. However, she tugged at the dress all evening in a desperate attempt at modesty. The event was a charity gala honoring Princess Grace of Monaco, who responded sympathetically when Diana confessed her embarrassment regarding the fashion debacle.

Right: At the time that she began seeing Prince Charles, Diana owned one long dress, one silk shirt, and one pair of good shoes. But this was not to last for long. Buckingham Palace presented her with a strict list of clothing requirements, which included four changes of clothes a day, from January to December. Nonetheless, Diana displayed a mind of her own, showing up at a polo match in a decidedly "non-royal" black sheep sweater, which quickly became a fashion fad.

*R*ight: Diana wept while seeing her husband-to-be off for a five-week tour of New Zealand, Australia, and Venezuela, just a month after their engagement. Her tears, however, were caused less by the parting than by her awareness of an intimate-sounding phone call that Charles had had with longtime friend Camilla Parker-Bowles before leaving for the airport.

*L*eft: Diana, with her "detective," or bodyguard, in tow, prepares to fly to Scotland to reunite with Charles upon his return from Australia. The young girl, who had enjoyed a substantial amount of freedom growing up, would not be traveling alone anymore.

*R*ight: The increasingly fashion-conscious Diana is caught in a pensive moment at Windsor Castle, just weeks before her wedding. The engagement period was trying, as she struggled to please Charles and satisfy the demands of the royal family, despite the lack of formal preparation for her new role.

*B*elow: Diana and Charles leave St. Paul's Cathedral after a wedding rehearsal, during which Diana—after endless trial runs of walking down the aisle under hot lights—dissolved into tears. Just before the rehearsal, Diana discovered a bracelet that Charles had bought for Camilla Parker-Bowles.

PART TWO

The Princess of Wales

On the morning of July 29, 1981, millions of sleepy-eyed Americans rose before dawn to turn on their televisions and enjoy one of the great feel-good moments of the twentieth century. The storybook wedding of the shy twenty-year-old aristocrat, Lady Diana Spencer, and the thirty-two-year-old Charles, Prince of Wales, heir to the crown of the United Kingdom, did not disappoint.

Sure, the winsome bride looked even younger than her years, almost like a girl playing dress-up. Sure, she appeared to be nervous. And sure, her dream wedding dress may have seemed a little over-the-top, like something out of the romance novels she adored—but we loved her all the more for it.

However, on that glorious day in July, no one, not even the principal players, knew that the fairy tale wouldn't have a happy ending. Diana was deeply in love, although she had already stumbled on disturbing clues alerting her to the fact that Charles's heart might not be hers alone. Charles, older and more realistic, seemed charmed by Diana's youth, her naïveté, her eagerness, her luminescence.

Nobody stopped to think at the time that the couple had almost nothing in common. It was their differences—her love for ABBA, his for *Tosca*; her love for Barbara Cartland romances and Danielle Steel potboilers, his for the works of Carl Gustav Jung and Laurens van der Post; her love for discos and shopping, his for polo and fishing—that would ultimately contribute to the demise of their marriage.

 bove: Lady Diana Spencer was not even a month past age twenty on her wedding day, July 29, 1981. A worldwide television audience of 750 million people watched the ceremony held in London's venerable St. Paul's Cathedral.

The other people would be incidental.

But that would all come later. After the wedding, the newly minted Princess of Wales was occupied with learning the responsibilities of her royal role. Her first steps were tentative and timid, and her first public speeches were given in the soft, quavering voice of a school-girl. But the camera loved her—and so did the people lining the streets everywhere she went. The press would make a career of following her, and for the most part, she would court the attention. Indeed, she would light up when photographers were around. In only a matter of months, she was firmly established as a global celebrity.

Left: Once a year, Diana would dutifully put on the uncomfortable tiara that had belonged to Charles's great grandmother, Queen Mary, to attend yet another opening of Parliament. The bejeweled headpiece, which was presented to Diana by Queen Elizabeth, consists of nineteen pearl droplets suspended from an intertwined lovers' knot of diamonds.

She also almost immediately became pregnant. In a way, of course, she was fulfilling her royal duty: producing an heir to the crown. But for an inexperienced teenager, anxious about her marriage, daily faced with the challenges of dealing with a voracious press and public, and deeply wounded by her parents' divorce, instant motherhood might not have been the best choice.

Above: While Diana continued to seem as though she were living out every little girl's dream, things were not as they appeared.

Indeed, Diana—suffering from an eating disorder, troubled by her husband's association with Camilla Parker-Bowles, and dogged by depression—became emotionally volatile as she awaited the birth of her first child. Prince Charles tried to get help for her, but ultimately, he just didn't understand what she was going through. After all, he had been taught from the cradle that emotions are best kept carefully in check.

If there was trouble brewing in the lives of the newlywed Waleses, however, the public didn't have a clue. Diana may have dissolved in tears before public appearances, but she glowed with youth and beauty the minute the cameras appeared. She made some fashion blunders in the beginning, but she learned quickly. One thing she didn't have to learn, though, was how to be empathetic. This quality came naturally to her, and the crowds adored her for it. They were drawn to her. In fact, when the Waleses would do royal walkabouts, people complained about being on Charles's side of the street. The Defender of the Faith began to resent being upstaged.

It wasn't long, though, before both members of the royal couple were upstaged, first by the sweet blonde child they called Wills, who was born in a hospital like any other baby, given loads of attention by his young parents, and taken along when they traveled overseas. And only two years later, a little ginger-haired boy named Harry arrived on the scene, looking as mischievous as his older brother looked angelic.

We rejoiced with the Prince and Princess of Wales as we admired the photographs of the picture-perfect family. Little did we know that the birth of Harry would mark the beginning of the end of Diana's fairy-tale marriage.

After the second prince's arrival, according to Diana, all marital relations ended. She began to sense that, having fulfilled her heir-producing duty, her use to Prince Charles had reached its conclusion. Of course, nothing is that simple. Charles had tried to understand and get help for his child bride. But ultimately, he appeared to became exasperated by her mercurial personality at home—and by her ability to grab the limelight away from home.

Prince Charles returned to his former mistress, Camilla Parker-Bowles, reigniting a relationship that he had ended upon his marriage. Camilla was different. Sharing many of the prince's interests, she was steady as a rock and loved horses and the country life. Moreover, she was exceedingly camera shy. She is the woman Charles probably should have married—but of course, at that time, she was already married.

Diana, longing for the affection that she had been deprived of for most of her life, began looking for love in all the wrong places . . . and finding it. Or rather what passed for it. There was a schoolgirl obsession with her bodyguard, Barry Mannakee. There was the riding instructor, James Hewitt, who claimed to love her, courted her on the sly for several years, charmed her sons, and ultimately dealt her the worst kind of betrayal; it was Hewitt who provided the material for Anna Pasternak's tell-all book *Princess in Love*, the story of his romance

Below: An older, more serious Princess Diana poses alone for this formal portrait. The girlish naïveté has been replaced by a gravity that becomes her.

Left: Throughout her life in the limelight, one of the most reliable indications that Princess Diana would be making a major shift in direction was a change in hairdo. Here, she sports a new style, the work of long-time hairdresser Sam McKnight, who would arrive at Kensington Palace every morning at nine o'clock to do her "do." The fresh look is clearly one of strength and independence.

with the world's most adored royal. And then, of course, there was car dealer James Gilbey, an old friend, who called her "Squidgy" and suffered the embarrassment of having his taped phone conversations with her printed in the tabloids. And there were others.

If her lovers disappointed, however, her millions of dedicated fans did not. She was by this point the most photographed woman in the world, and far and away the most popular member of the royal family. She was the person that mothers wanted their daughters to emulate. No matter where Diana traveled, people would turn out by the thousands to see her. They reached out to shake her hand, told her that they loved her, and gave her the confidence to grow up.

And grow up she did. As she neared thirty, Diana changed direction.

The little girl who had described herself as "thick as a plank" proved that she was anything but. She began to master the nuances of world affairs; she became involved in a growing number of charities; she cared for AIDS patients and orphans; she worked out and reached out. And she looked better than she ever had in her life.

Ironically, just as Diana was coming into her own, her marriage was coming to an end. For some time, Prince Charles had been residing at his country house, Highgrove, just nine miles (14.5km) from Camilla's home. Meanwhile, Diana, her beloved boys off at school, remained alone at Kensington Palace. The Prince and Princess of Wales were communicating by memo.

It was a desperately unhappy situation. Nonetheless, there were still royal tours to complete and Diana doggedly went on them. But when we look at the photographs from these last tours—Diana posing alone at the Taj Mahal, Diana alone in front of the pyramids at Giza—a change is apparent. Perhaps most telling of all is the image of Diana turning her head away as the prince attempts to kiss her in front of photographers.

By the end of 1992, the situation had gone too far. Both parties were privately consulting lawyers, and at last they consulted the queen. Their existing separation was about to be formalized.

On December 9, 1992, Prime Minister John Major formally announced to the House of Commons—and to reporters from all over the world—that the Prince and Princess of Wales had decided to part. The world now knew what Diana had known for a while: there was to be no happily ever after for her and her prince.

Above: Diana's wedding gown, designed by Elizabeth and David Emanuel, contained forty-four yards (40m) of ivory silk taffeta trimmed with ten thousand mother-of-pearl sequins and pearls. A panel of lace once worn by Queen Mary served as "something old," while a gold-and-diamond horseshoe (a gift from Diana's father) sewn into the skirt of the gown fulfilled the role of "something new." Diana borrowed the Spencer family tiara and wore a pair of earrings belonging to her mother. A tiny blue bow sewn inside the skirt of the gown provided "something blue."

Above: Despite the fact that both the bride and groom made slight errors during their vows—Diana said her husband's four names in the wrong order and Charles stated, "All *thy* goods with thee I share," rather than "All *my* worldly goods with thee I share"—the royal couple was pronounced man and wife.

Above: At Buckingham Palace, the new princess—still clutching her bouquet of gardenias, roses, orchids, lilies of the valley, freesia, myrtle, veronica, and stephanotis—stops to share a special word with her youngest bridesmaid, five-year-old Clementine Hambro. Diana's new mother-in-law, Queen Elizabeth II, looks on.

Above: "We want Charlie!" "We want Di!" screamed the throngs of people waiting beneath the balcony at Buckingham Palace. The crowd was rewarded with five separate appearances by Charles and Diana, their parents, and their attendants.

Above: "Kiss her, kiss her," the crowd demanded. Finally, at the urging of Prince Andrew, Prince Charles broke all royal precedent, kissing his new bride on the lips in public.

Above: As the royal couple pose for their official wedding photograph, it is difficult to tell who is *more* royal. Indeed, Diana's father reportedly wondered aloud if a Windsor was good enough to marry a Spencer. Diana's family had played a key role in putting the Hanoverians, the German princes who became the House of Windsor, on the throne. No stranger to royal blood, Diana was descended from Kings James I, Charles I, and Charles II.

Right: After spending the wedding night at the Mountbatten family estate at Broadlands, the couple flew to Gibraltar, where they boarded the royal yacht *Britannia* for a sixteen-day honeymoon cruise through the Mediterranean, Aegean, and Red seas. During their cruise, the couple swam, snorkeled, watched videos of the wedding, and exchanged love notes.

Left: Storm clouds were never far away, however. During the trip, two photographs of Camilla dropped from Charles's personal calendar, landing at Diana's feet. And as Charles was dressing for a formal dinner with Egyptian president Anwar Sadat, Diana noticed him putting on cuff links that contained intertwined Cs. Charles admitted that the cuff links had been a friendly gift from Camilla, but said that he had ended his intimate relationship with her, as per his promise to his father.

Left: Charles and Diana continued their honeymoon at Balmoral Castle in Scotland, where they attended services at Crathie Church (the sermon text was, rather unsubtly, "Go and bear fruit"). Later, they posed for the press. When asked about married life, Diana gamely replied, "I highly recommend it."

Right: Diana's first public tour took her to Wales. Crowds followed her wherever she went, sometimes waiting for as long as six hours in the pouring rain to catch a glimpse of her.

bove: Diana's first public appearance in London was the State Opening of Parliament on November 4, 1981. In full formal dress, she sported a heavy diamond tiara, a gift from the queen. The next day, the Palace announced that a baby would be arriving in June.

ight: Though she was suffering from all-day morning sickness, Diana still made public appearances. Here, she is pictured visiting the Scilly Isles, where she continued to charm the crowds and the press. She loved the attention—something she may have been lacking at home.

Left: Charles, an avid polo player and hunter, was deeply disappointed by Diana's unwillingness to ride (her reluctance stemmed from two serious falls she had had as a child). In fact, the "sport of kings" plays such an important role in Charles's life that the birth of his first son was scheduled—with labor to be induced—for a day that wouldn't interfere with a polo match.

Right: The eagerly awaited heir to the throne, Prince William of Wales, arrived at 9:03 P.M. on Monday, June 21, 1982, at St. Mary's Hospital in Paddington. Ever conscious of the press, twenty-year-old Diana had had her hair done before leaving for the hospital. Charles remained with her throughout the labor and birth. Here, she stands with her family, looking fresh as a flower only twenty-one hours after giving birth.

Right: Less than a month after Prince William's birth, the beautiful young princess had a formal portrait taken to mark her twenty-first birthday. The photographer, Lord Snowdon, is the ex-husband of the late Princess Margaret, one of the few "royals" that Diana genuinely enjoyed. Diana lunched with Sarah Ferguson on her birth-day, then looked at some of the two thousand birthday cards and forty bags of gifts that arrived.

Below: The Archbishop of Canterbury officiated at the christening of Prince William Arthur Philip Louis, held August 4, 1982. Diana, who was suffering from severe postpartum depression, felt that she was excluded from many of the photographs. She did look frail, having lost forty pounds (18kg) since giving birth. There was talk of suicide attempts during these dark days, but Diana pulled herself together, vowing to soldier on for Wills.

Above: Despite marital and emotional troubles, Diana and Charles took much delight in their little blonde boy, bragging about his sweet nature and how long he would sleep at night. While William, shown here at six months, had a nanny, Diana was far more involved in his infant care than is typical among the royals.

Above: On March 20, 1983, the Prince and Princess of Wales, and William, set out for a six-week tour of Australia and New Zealand. Their first stop was the remote—and blisteringly hot—Alice Springs in the outback.

Above: Their arduous travels, and their shared delight in their young son, seemed to bring the couple closer together. Diana allotted three hours every morning to spend with her child before beginning her official round of appointments. She was exercising hard and seemed more in control of her emotions. Here, the infant heir to the throne awaits his second Christmas.

Right: On Valentine's Day of 1984, Charles and Diana announced that they were going to have another child. The pregnancy ended up being somewhat easier this time, and Diana later described the summer months before the birth as the most intimate time she ever had with her husband. She continued to appear before public and press, attending many headache-inducing "tiara functions," as she would call them.

Left: Both Charles and Diana longed for a daughter this time, but Diana had early on seen an ultrasound that showed she was carrying another son. Nevertheless, there was much happiness when Prince Henry (Harry) arrived on September 15, 1984.

Right: The Prince and Princess of Wales pose for a formal portrait with their children. Diana was thrilled with her sons, but was privately concerned that having produced the requisite "heir and a spare," she would no longer be of use to her husband. Indeed, royal watchers were already gossiping that Charles had returned to former mistress Camilla Parker-Bowles in a less than platonic way.

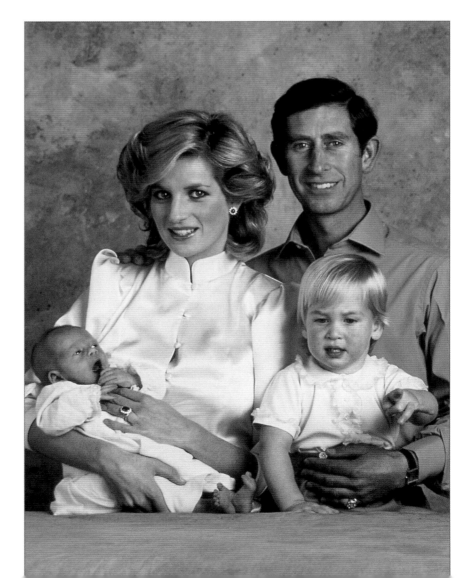

Left: While Prince Harry was blossoming into an adorable child, the British aristocracy was abuzz with rumors that the Waleses' marriage was truly in trouble. Ultimately, the royal couple took to the airwaves to refute the charges, with Diana saying that she felt "wounded" by the gossip and Charles admitting to having become more of an eccentric with age.

Right: Still in love with love, the media grasped at every straw. When Diana and Charles exchanged a terse kiss on the polo field, the photo appeared in newspapers around the world. It seemed as though the prince and princess were trying to hold things together. In reality, however, they were sleeping in separate bedrooms.

*L*eft: While Diana remained deeply committed to mothering, finding great fulfillment in nurturing her children, she felt that she needed something more in her life. She began to reach out for some genuine affection.

*R*ight: Diana appeared to find the affection she was craving, at least for a time, in the concern offered by her detective Barry Mannakee, whose job it was to shadow her everywhere. Mannakee, married and from a working-class background, comforted Diana in her distress but was alarmed by the depth of her neediness. While the relationship may have remained purely paternal, Mannakee was abruptly, and unexpectedly, transferred from his post. When he died in a motorcycle accident not long after, Diana became deeply suspicious.

Above: Diana and Charles continued to tour together, making a visit to Rome in April 1985 that included a tour of the Sistine Chapel and a meeting with Pope John Paul II.

Above: Diana was thrilled to learn that she and Charles would make a return visit to Australia, the country that had welcomed her so warmly as a young bride. Still hoping to make things work, she believed that the time alone with Charles would be valuable. Unfortunately, she upstaged him all the way. When the couple was asked to perform in Melbourne, Charles played a botched piece on the cello. Diana followed with a perfectly executed Rachmaninoff concerto on the piano.

Above: When Irish pop singer Bob Geldof produced the sixteen-hour-long LIVE AID concert—which ran simultaneously in London and Philadelphia on July 13, 1985—Charles and Diana were front row center at Wembley Stadium. Doubtless Charles was doing his royal duty, but Diana loved the music. LIVE AID ultimately raised more than $100 million for famine relief in Ethiopia. Diana's presence certainly didn't hurt. It's said that whenever she appeared at a benefit, the receipts doubled.

bove: Diana and John Travolta, who was invited at her request, dominated the dance floor at a special White House ball held on November 9, 1985. Diana was a vision in an ink-blue gown that later sold at auction for nearly $250,000. Travolta gave the princess a ten out of ten rating as a dancer.

 Above: In 1986, twenty-five-year-old Diana decided that if she could conquer her fear of horses, she could successfully compete with the horse-loving Camilla Parker-Bowles and win her husband back. She retained James Hewitt, a captain in the cavalry, to give her riding lessons. Soon, during their early morning rides, she was confiding in her instructor, who also taught William and Harry.

 Above: Diana and Charles took to the road again in the autumn of 1986, this time to the Persian Gulf. They toured Oman, Qatar, Bahrain, and Saudi Arabia, where royalty charmed royalty.

Left: Here, Diana makes a formal appearance in Riyadh, Saudi Arabia. After this stop, she returned to England while Charles continued on to Cyprus. With the prince away, Diana invited James Hewitt to a private dinner (sans staff) at Kensington Palace. Thus began an affair that would last for several years.

 bove: Diana found great comfort with Hewitt, who charmed her, provided an escape valve for her, and even took her away for quiet weekends at his mother's home in Devon. Later, Hewitt would betray her, working with writer Anna Pasternak on a tell-all book about their affair.

Left: There wasn't a pair of polka-dot socks left in any store in Great Britain the day after Diana was photographed in these flashy red-and-white anklets. While she often said that she wished people would stop talking about what she wore, clothes were very important to her. The young girl who had come to marriage with hardly a dress to her name owned more than 80 suits, 144 evening gowns, and 50 dresses—with accessories to match—by 1987. She played an invaluable role in promoting British fashion and was said to have been worth the equivalent of tens of millions of dollars to the industry.

Right: Charles and Diana enjoyed some royal relief as the media turned its attention toward the new kid on the block, redheaded Sarah Ferguson, a longtime friend (and fourth cousin) of Diana. After Sarah's marriage to Prince Andrew in 1986, she and Diana became inseparable for a time. The press, however, was not always kind, viewing the women's behavior—as in this instance at Ascot, where the two were using their umbrellas like cattle prods—as silly and hedonistic.

 bove: By 1988, the press had unequivocally declared the '80s the "Decade of Diana." She was consistently rated favorite member of the royal family.

Right: As she matured, Diana became increasingly interested in charitable causes. Here, compassionate as always, she holds a serious conversation with two-year-old Ashley Scott. At the time, the young girl was living with her father at City Roads, a North London crisis center for drug addicts. Diana was there to open the new parent and child unit.

 Above: Still, this lover of popular culture was not too busy to meet the icons of the time. Here, the Princess of Wales chats with the King of Pop. While Diana listed Elton John and ABBA among her favorite musicians, Charles has always preferred opera.

 bove: Even the French press swooned over Diana, calling her November 1988 visit to attend the Armistice ceremonies "a triumphant tour." Charles was also in attendance.

ight: By 1989, the Waleses seemed to have settled into their new way of living separately together, and the gossip mills slowed. Here, Diana, looking striking in red, inspects the troops at Dartmouth.

elow: Diana poses with her family at the marriage of her beloved younger brother Charles, Viscount Althorp, to Victoria Lockwood, on September 16, 1989. The princess noted the bride's extreme thinness and realized that she, too, suffered from an eating disorder. Sadly, this marriage did not last, imploding amid accusations of the viscount's infidelities.

Above: Looking regal as ever, the princess turned heads at a banquet honoring Nigeria's military ruler Ibrahim Babangida. Diana, who would visit Nigeria during the following year, was becoming increasingly interested in the world she saw during her travels. Ultimately, she expressed her desire to become a sort of ambassador for Great Britain, noting that wherever she traveled, at least ninety British photographers followed her; she thought this publicity could be put to good use.

Above: Diana, herself having come from a broken home, struggled to protect William and Harry from the arguments between her and Charles. Here, she walks the boys to Wetherby, their London day school.

Right: In late 1989, to Diana's sorrow, James Hewitt accepted a two-year posting to Germany. However, she had already become interested in her old friend James Gilbey, of the Gilbey gin family. Her sentimental telephone conversations with Gilbey, who called her Squidgy, and Charles's more openly sexual and emotional ones with Camilla would secretly be recorded and later released to the press.

Above: Despite ongoing concern about her marriage, Diana's press continued to be fabulous, except for an occasional carp about her annual six-figure clothing budget. But her many fans—not to mention the press—always expected to see her in something new, and indeed, the princess seldom appeared in the same outfit more than two or three times. Here, she looks radiant in satin and lace.

Above: By 1990, Diana had taken voice and media training so that she would be ready to meet the press on its own terms. If she ever harked back to the early promises made by Charles and his parents—that the intense scrutiny by the press would stop after the wedding—she now knew that such a concept was an idle dream. Here, she does one of her famous walkabouts, this time in Nigeria.

Right: In October 1990, Diana jetted off to Washington, D.C., to attend a benefit for the London City Ballet held at the Department of Commerce. Wearing an eye-popping red evening gown, she dazzled those around her. Diana loved haute couture and her couturiers loved her, delighting in her common touch. One claimed to have returned to his studio once to find the princess, early for a fitting, contentedly washing his dishes.

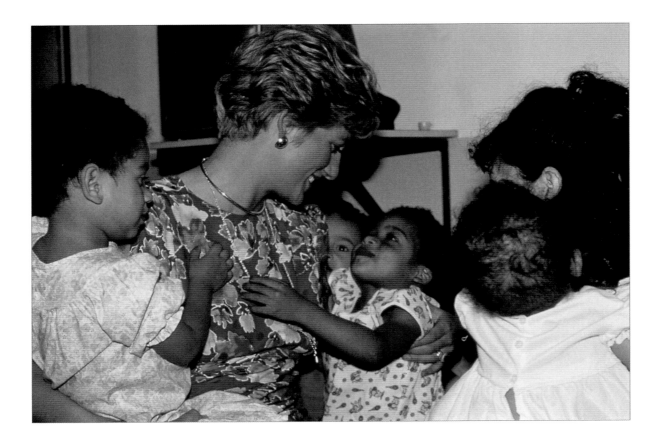

 bove: Diana shares her warmth and maternal touch with a group of ill children in Brazil in the spring of 1991. During that year, she significantly stepped up her work with charities, increasing the number of organizations she supported from sixty to more than one hundred.

bove: Becoming increasingly used to shouldering the responsibility of the children by herself, Diana took Prince Harry on a wet and wild excursion to Thorpe Park, outside London. Still young enough to act like a kid, mom joined in the fun.

Above: Diana rides the ski lift with William and Harry on a spring vacation in Lech, Austria. The tabloids had been closely monitoring Charles's absence from family life, and on this occasion, the *Daily Mail* trumpeted the headline "WISH YOU WERE HERE PAPA."

Above: Charles and Diana attend a victory parade for the heroes of the Gulf War. Just a few weeks earlier, Charles had received a clobbering from the press due to an incident involving William. The boy, having received a depressed fracture from a hit in the head with a golf club, required surgery. As Diana paced and worried during the complex operation, she noticed that Charles had disappeared. He had gone to the opera.

Above: James Hewitt, by this time out of the picture, had left the little princes with a lasting legacy, a love of horses and riding, as shown here. Diana, about to turn thirty and celebrate her tenth wedding anniversary, had embarked on a secret project—a series of taped interviews for writer Andrew Morton that would save her side of the marital story for posterity.

 bove: The transformation of child bride into mature stateswoman was almost complete as Diana reached age thirty. With her children at school, she turned her interests increasingly toward charities and world issues.

Above: Diana does an informal walkabout at Barnardos, a charity serving the poor in London's crime-ridden East End. The princess had expressed a desire to start a Princess of Wales Trust to raise funds for her favorite charities. She was stopped by her husband, however, who feared it would pull cash away from his own Prince's Trust.

Above: In February 1992, just as her biography by Andrew Morton was being delivered to the publisher, Diana and Charles embarked upon an extensive trip to India. While in Calcutta, Diana visited Mother Teresa's order, the Missionaries of Charity. Diana was very fond of the beloved nun, and would later be buried holding a rosary given to her by Mother Teresa. Here, Diana looks regal as ever at a formal event in Delhi.

Left: Diana turns her head away as Charles attempts to kiss her at the conclusion of a polo match in Jaipur. The press had a field day with the seemingly deliberate slight.

Below: Perhaps attempting to make amends after the India trip, Charles organized another skiing vacation to Lech the following month. While there, Diana received word that her father, who had been suffering from pneumonia, had died of a heart attack. She wished to return home alone, but Charles insisted on accompanying her. The tension was highly apparent by the time they arrived in England.

*R*ight: Diana and Harry engage in some museum-going, just a month after her father's death. Diana felt vulnerable without the protection of Earl Spencer. She would feel even more so in August, with the publication of the text of the infamous "Squidgygate" tapes in the London tabloid the *Sun*.

*B*elow: As if emphasizing her solitary stance in the world, Diana poses alone in front of the pyramids at Giza during a May 1992 trip to Egypt. The last time she had been there was on her honeymoon.

Left: In June 1992, London's *Sunday Times* began to serialize Andrew Morton's *Diana: Her True Story*. The world was stunned as it read about Diana's troubled life, her bulimia, her suicide attempts, and Charles's ongoing adultery with Camilla Parker-Bowles. While the furor grew, Diana diligently continued with her royal duties.

Below: Diana was an early and intense advocate for AIDS patients, having been brought to the cause when one of her friends became ill. Here, she visits an AIDS hospice, extending a royal hand to one of the residents.

Right: All eyes are on Diana in this picture taken during her November 1992 trip with Charles to Korea. The tour was a personal and public relations disaster. The pair made such little effort to be pleasant to one another that the press started calling them "the glums."

Below: It was not long after the couple's return to England that a shocking announcement was made. On December 9, 1992, Prime Minister John Major told the House of Commons that the couple would be separating.

bove: Lord Snowdon again captured Diana on film, this time in a formal portrait that reflects a more independent, mature, and determined woman.

PART THREE

On Her Own

The newly liberated Princess Diana appeared to be some kind of sweet fairy godmother, waving a wand of goodwill and healing over the less fortunate of the world. As she delivered speeches about the causes she was championing, the striking woman, who had once been so timid and unsure, demonstrated the poise and confidence of the superstar she had become. But it was because her concern for the poor, oppressed, and ill so clearly came from her heart that people everywhere responded to her. She had a tremendous amount of compassion and a remarkable ability to empathize.

Buckingham Palace, however, had had more than enough of that goodwill. Any thought that the formal announcement of Charles and Diana's separation would solve the "Diana problem" and cause the public's attention and affection to return to Prince Charles was quickly dispelled. During the first six days of March in 1993, for example, Diana received 3,500 column inches (8,890cm) of press, almost all of it glowing. Prince Charles, by contrast, earned 300 less-than-heartwarming column inches (762cm).

But Diana was beginning to feel the strain of the constant media attention and the royal family's disapproval. And she was tired. To everyone's surprise, on December 3, 1993, Diana announced her intention to withdraw from public life, ending her statement with the warm words, "Your kindness and affection have carried me through some of the most difficult periods, and always your love and care have eased the journey." Less than a week after the startling announcement, the Archdeacon of York commented on the radio that the Prince of Wales was not fit to be king, given that he had broken his vows of marriage and his vows to God.

Diana didn't put a halt to all of her public efforts, but reduced the number of causes she was supporting from about 120 to 5: AIDS, leprosy, the homeless, Great Ormond Street Children's Hospital (where Prince William had had his successful surgery), and the elderly. She was still covering a broad canvas.

Meanwhile, she was spending as much time as possible with her sons. Diana was the parent who would take them to the movies and McDonald's and host their sleep-overs during school vacation. It was Diana who ordered her children not to behave in a high-handed way in public. And it was Diana who would joke with them and laugh when they teased her by calling her "Squidgy."

In 1994, Charles, never as media savvy as his estranged wife and deeply disturbed by all of the negative public sentiment toward him, made another gross error by telling his story on television. He did an on-air interview with palace-insider Jonathan Dimbleby, during which he admitted to having committed adultery with Camilla Parker-Bowles during his marriage. He also said that Camilla had been the "mainstay" of his life for years, adding somewhat defiantly that she would continue as such.

Charles's appearance got results, though certainly not the kind he was hoping for. Any sympathy that had not already gone Diana's way went to her now. The queen and Prince Philip were fuming, and Andrew Parker-Bowles sued Camilla for divorce. Diana, meanwhile, had managed to steal the spotlight once again. Even as Charles was on the air, she appeared at a London fund-raising dinner in a to-die-for off-the-shoulder dress. Looking positively beautiful, she appeared in virtually every newspaper the following day.

Ultimately, Diana took to television, too, appearing on *Panorama*, one of England's top-rated shows. Dressed in a subdued black suit, her makeup muted, she looked serious and sad. When interviewer Martin Bashir asked her about her failed marriage, she touched viewers' hearts with the simple statement, "There were three of us in this marriage, so it was a bit crowded."

Soon after, Diana received a letter from Queen Elizabeth II requesting that she and Charles divorce. The following February, the princess was commanded to appear before Her Majesty and Prince Charles. During the brief meeting, the queen—who had refused to allow her own sister to marry a divorced man—elicited Diana's agreement to an uncontested divorce. Diana would later say that it was the saddest day of her life.

In the end, Diana received a large settlement, and—of greatest concern to her—joint custody of her sons. In return, she promised never to write or speak about the monarchy, the prince, or her marriage again.

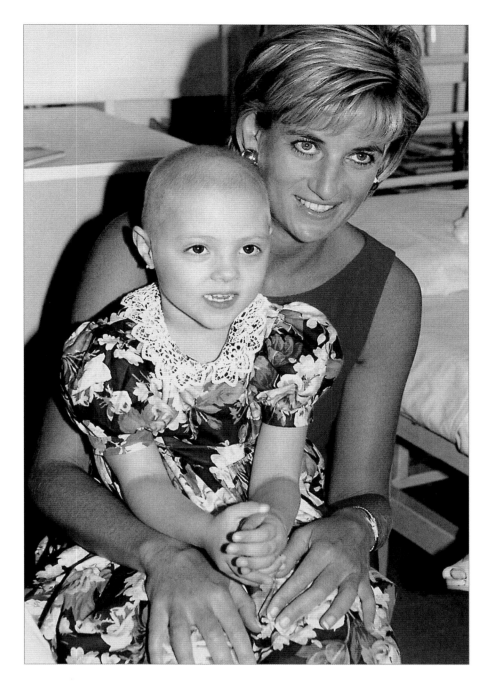

Right: Diana reaches out to a child suffering from cancer at Northwick Park Hospital near London. She was volunteering for fewer causes by this point, but she was making a greater impact on those to which she devoted her time.

She did lose one battle, though. While she succeeded in keeping the title Princess of Wales, she would no longer be referred to as Her Royal Highness. Now, according to strict royal protocol, Diana would be obliged to bow before her own sons. Both boys felt for their mother, and Prince William made it his business to comfort her.

Diana continued her charity work, visiting the poor neighborhoods of New York City with Mother Teresa, making surprise visits to cancer clinics and AIDS hospices, and speaking out against the use of land mines. Although she had her own problems, she reached out to those whose needs were greater.

Throughout this whole painful period, she fell in love, again and again. There was the married Oliver Hoare, a wealthy dealer in Islamic art—and friend of Prince Charles—who tried to comfort her when her marriage broke down. Diana responded with an ongoing obsession. When Hoare's wife started to tire of the twenty or so anonymous phone calls that would

Above: During June 1997 in Washington, D.C., Diana presented a stirring speech to the assembled media about the worldwide problem of land mines. While the attention that she brought to this cause was invaluable, some Conservative members of Parliament were furious that she had taken on such a serious and politically charged issue.

come to her home every week, she convinced the police to track them. The authorities were astounded to find that they came from Kensington Palace.

Then there was the handsome, and deeply compassionate, Hasnat Khan, a Pakistani heart surgeon whom Diana met through friends. He was in England to study new surgical techniques to use in treating the poorest of his fellow Pakistanis. Diana was taken with his humanitarian spirit. But again, the relationship did not work out.

And, of course, there was Emad "Dodi" Al Fayed. The doomed lovers met when Diana and her sons were vacationing on the yacht of Dodi's father, Mohamed Al Fayed, the wealthy Egyptian businessman who owns, among other things, the famous London department store Harrods. Known as a playboy, Dodi—engaged to an American fashion model at the time— was charming and fun. And he, like Diana, knew what it was like to go through the divorce of one's parents.

There was an instant rapport. While the press went to town about the fact that she was dating another Muslim, Diana fell head over heels in love. Dodi reciprocated, and romance blossomed.

But it was not to last for long. On the final weekend of August 1997, the happy couple was in Paris, where they had dinner at the Ritz, owned by Dodi's father. As they attempted to leave the hotel, they found that the photographers and crowds were so intense that it would be almost impossible to escape. Mohamed Al Fayed urged the two to stay at the hotel, but they refused. They tried sending out a decoy car, but the crowds saw through the ruse. When Diana and Dodi finally exited through the service entrance, a parade of photographers, several on motorcycles, followed them. Their driver, Henri Paul, decided to avoid the Champs-Elysée, where the paparazzi would have been able to take pictures of the couple through the car windows. Instead, he headed for the Alma tunnel.

But Henri Paul was intoxicated and driving at a high speed. He hit a slow-moving automobile, and the car carrying Diana and Dodi spun desperately out of control, ultimately crashing into a concrete wall. Dodi Fayed died instantly. Henri Paul also lost his life. Diana's bodyguard was seriously wounded.

Diana was still alive at the scene, but died on the operating table the following morning, August 31, at 4:00 A.M. People across the globe went into mourning for this woman who had shown so much vulnerability and compassion during her brief life.

The world had lost its princess.

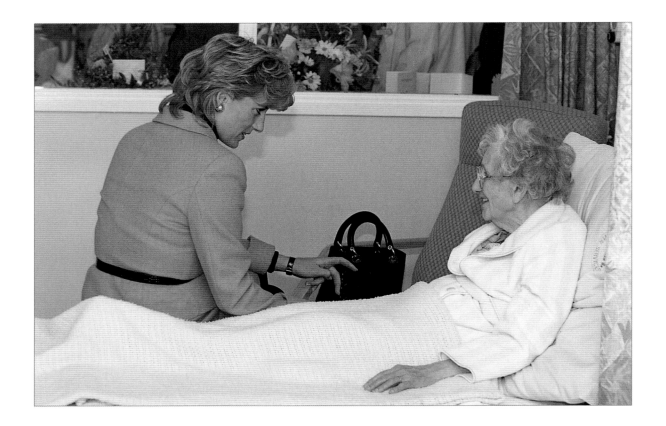

Above: The mature Diana, her husband gone and sons away at school, threw herself into an ever-increasing number of charitable causes, including AIDS, leprosy, and the Red Cross. Here, she visits with an elderly patient at Liverpool Women's Hospital. The people Diana spent time with were always amazed by her easy and unaffected manner. But Buckingham Palace was becoming increasingly uncomfortable with Diana's high profile following the official separation.

Left: The royal family denied so many of Diana's requests to appear at major charity events that the *Evening Standard* wondered in print why the Windsors didn't just put the Princess of Wales under house arrest. Weary of it all, the emotionally fragile princess announced her wish to withdraw from public life in December 1993. She cut her schedule from 198 royal events that year to just 10 in 1994.

Right: On June 29, 1994, Prince Charles told thirteen million BBC viewers that he had committed adultery with Camilla Parker-Bowles during his marriage. That same evening Diana, aware that the interview was taking place and determined to look like a survivor, appeared at a London charity event in one of her most spectacular, and becoming, dresses. Her photograph was everywhere the next day. Despite this moment of victory, she was worried about the effect that Charles's revelations would have on William and Harry.

Below: While Diana was capable of using the paparazzi to communicate her side of the story, she increasingly became their prisoner. Photographers followed her every step, knowing that one good shot could mean a small fortune. Diana had officially given up her security guards in early 1994, hoping that it would give her a chance at a more normal life, but she quickly learned that that freedom sometimes meant feeling dangerously exposed on the street.

Left: Even while she was trying to keep a low profile, nights on the town meant photos in the papers. And those papers were almost certain to be the tabloids, which Diana, ever the populist, favored. She often joked with an elderly photographer from the *Sun*, who used to complain when Diana wore the same dress too often, and she brought him medicine when he became ill. In the autumn of 1994, she quietly resumed public life.

Right: On a four-day tour of Japan in February 1995, Diana's popularity soared. During that same year, she also made visits to Russia and Argentina. By this point, Diana was stating that, as a result of therapy, she was back on her feet, yet in reality she was also seeking treatment for her continuing struggle with bulimia. Just months earlier, the revealing tell-all book about James Hewitt's romance with the princess had been published.

bove: The Waleses often appeared as a viable—and even happy—family unit at special events, such as this formal occasion commemorating the fiftieth anniversary of the end of World War II in Europe. Yet resentments were boiling just below the surface, making this show of family amity ring false.

elow: Always athletic, Diana shines as she and William take to the court in the Mothers and Sons Tennis Match at Ludgrove School, the Berkshire boarding school attended by both her boys.

On Her Own

Right: The whole family turned out for thirteen-year-old William's first day at Eton, one of Great Britain's best and oldest schools. Diana missed her boys deeply during their absences, but kept them with her through the many photographs she displayed in her Kensington Palace apartment.

Left: As Diana built up confidence in her new position, her clothes became more and more revealing, as evidenced by this dress worn to a private screening of the 1995 film *Apollo 13*. Her disciplined regimen of exercise— swimming, tennis, dance, and workouts at the gym— had resulted in an hourglass 36-26-36 figure.

Right: A pensive Diana walks through Kensington. After Diana's confessional television interview with Martin Bashir in November 1995—during which the princess admitted to having had an affair with James Hewitt—Queen Elizabeth demanded that the couple divorce. The media then flew into a frenzy, speculating about Diana's future.

Above: A triumphant Diana headed to New York in December 1995 to receive the Humanitarian of the Year Award from former Secretary of State Henry Kissinger at a dinner benefiting the United Cerebral Palsy Foundation. Decked out in a sequined dress by designer Jacques Azagury, she received a standing ovation for her charitable work.

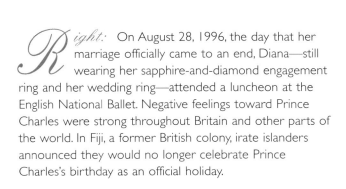

Left: Diana attends a charity banquet sponsored by Pakistani cricket player Imran Khan and his wife, twenty-two-year-old Jemima Goldsmith, daughter of billionaire British financier Jimmy Goldsmith. Khan enlisted Diana to help raise funds for the cancer hospital he founded in Pakistan in honor of his mother, who died of the disease.

Right: On August 28, 1996, the day that her marriage officially came to an end, Diana—still wearing her sapphire-and-diamond engagement ring and her wedding ring—attended a luncheon at the English National Ballet. Negative feelings toward Prince Charles were strong throughout Britain and other parts of the world. In Fiji, a former British colony, irate islanders announced they would no longer celebrate Prince Charles's birthday as an official holiday.

Above: Divorced just a month, Diana strides through Heathrow Airport to board the Concorde to New York, where she would attend a celebrity-packed series of events in support of the Nina Hyde Center for Breast Cancer Research. Her gait reflects her new sense of being completely in charge of her life.

*A*bove: Diana's U.S. visit began with a breakfast with Hillary Clinton at the Nina Hyde Center. Diana liked the first lady, admiring her strong personality and unwillingness to bow to pressure—qualities that Diana felt she shared with Mrs. Clinton.

*L*eft: That evening, Diana served as honorary chair of the Breast Cancer Super Sale, also for the Nina Hyde Center. She is flanked here by cochairs Ralph Lauren and *Vogue* editor in chief Anna Wintour. Surrounded by glamorous people in fashionable black, Diana shone in a romantic white lace gown by Catherine Walker. In the course of the evening, she danced with Colin Powell and Calvin Klein, jokingly telling Klein that she liked his underwear.

Above: Just three months later, Diana was back in New York to attend one of the major social events of the season, the Metropolitan Museum of Art's gala benefit for its Costume Institute. She appeared in a highly controversial slip dress, part of John Galliano's couture collection for Dior. The press carped that the garment wasn't made for a well-endowed woman with ties to royalty, and Diana later confessed that she had had to lose three pounds in three days to fit into it. She went to the event at the invitation of her good friend Liz Tilberis, editor of *Harper's Bazaar*, who was already suffering from the ovarian cancer that would take her life.

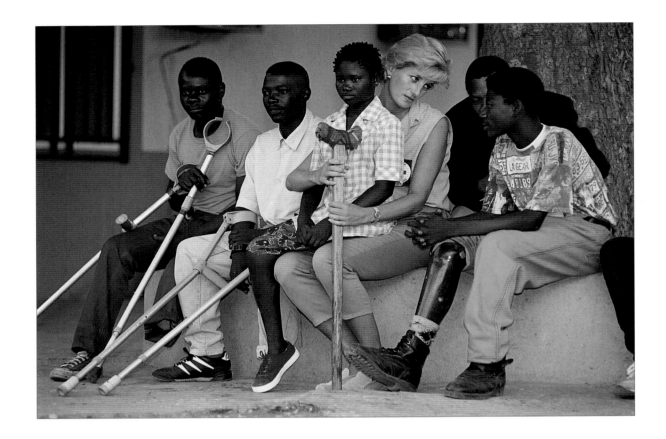

Above: Diana became increasingly interested in the issue of land mines, partly through her association with Lord Richard Attenborough, who had directed and produced a film, *In Love and War*, about the disastrous impact of these devices on people's lives. She agreed to raise money for the cause, and traveled to Angola with the Red Cross, where she visited the I.C.R.C. Orthopaedic Workshop and Centre, meeting with young men who had lost limbs to mines. While there, she also appeared in a segment of the popular British television show *Heart of the Matter*, putting on protective clothing and following a bomb-disposal team through a minefield.

Left: When she encountered illness and death, Diana reached out. People have often commented that she was never put off by the smells and sights of disease, that she always managed to see past them. Here, she holds a young cancer patient in Imran Khan's hospital in Lahore, Pakistan. While in that country, she also visited the family of Pakistani heart surgeon Hasnat Khan (no relation to Imran), with whom she was having a romantic relationship.

Right: The Windsors were out in full force to observe Prince William's confirmation on March 9, 1997. This was, perhaps, a more important event for William than for most fourteen-year-olds. After all, when he becomes king, he will also become head of the Church of England. On this special day, for the first time in a long period, the tension between Charles and Diana seemed absent, and the two genuinely appeared to get along.

Left: At the suggestion of Prince William, who had gotten the idea while watching his mother dig through her wardrobe, Diana decided to auction off her old gowns for charity. Here, she attends the preview party at Christie's in New York. The actual bidding would start the following day. In the end, seventy-nine of her gowns were sold, raising $3.26 million for AIDS and cancer charities.

Right: During June 1997, Diana traveled to New York to meet with one of her great heroes, Mother Teresa, founder of the Missionaries of Charity, a Catholic order that serves the poorest of the poor. Here, in an impoverished section of the Bronx, the princess and the nun share warm greetings before visiting an AIDS hospice together. Ironically, the two universally revered female figures would die within a week of each other later that summer.

Left: On Diana's thirty-sixth birthday, she was a guest of honor at a gala hosted by Chanel to celebrate the centennial of London's Tate Gallery. She wore a figure-flattering Jacques Azagury gown and the emerald-and-diamond choker that Queen Elizabeth had given her when she married Charles. Diana was looking forward to her upcoming vacation in the south of France, where she and the boys would be guests of Egyptian businessman Mohamed Al Fayed, owner of Harrods.

Below: After flying to the Riviera on the private Harrods plane, Diana and Harry took to the blue Mediterranean waters—with twelve-year-old Harry in the driver's seat. Al Fayed had the royals protected by his own forty-eight armed security guards, allowing the children and their mother to feel safe. Two days later, the businessman's son Dodi appeared, and he and Diana developed an instant rapport that quickly escalated into true romance.

Right: Despite concerns about her safety, on August 8, 1997, Diana journeyed to Bosnia, a nation that is reported to have more than one million land mines, most of them not noted on any map. Traveling with her loyal butler, Paul Burrell, she visited dozens of patients maimed by mines, spending long hours in small, poorly equipped hospitals.

Left: In late August, Diana and Dodi embarked on Mohamed Al Fayed's yacht *Jonikal* for a private Mediterranean cruise. Solitude was limited, however, as they were constantly being followed by the press, who kept high-powered lenses focused on them from morning 'til night. Nonetheless, love blossomed, with Diana telling friends that this could be the real thing. It was a time of great promise. Almost unimaginably, a week later, on August 30, Dodi and Diana would have their romantic dinner at the Ritz, to be followed by their fatal race through the Alma tunnel.

On Her Own

Left: Just as they had tuned in for the fairy-tale wedding sixteen years earlier, the world watched as Princes Charles, William, and Harry, and Diana's brother, the ninth Earl Spencer, followed Diana's coffin into Westminster Abbey for her funeral service on September 6, 1997.

Below: Some of the ten thousand tons of flowers left in Diana's honor adorned the front of Buckingham Palace. A similar sea of color completely covered the lawn at Kensington Palace. While the people of England poured their hearts out in grief over the loss of the woman whom Prime Minister Tony Blair dubbed the "People's Princess," the residents of Buckingham Palace remained surprisingly silent in their response to the tragedy.

Above: In one of the last formal portraits ever taken of her, Diana looks regal and sure of herself. She had mastered the difficult job of being the "celebrity royal," she had made a tremendous impact on charitable causes and individuals around the world, and she had raised two wonderful sons. Today, she continues to live in the hearts of the many people she affected and influenced.

Bibliography

Adler, Bill. *Diana: A Portrait in Her Own Words*. New York: William Morrow and Company, Inc., 1999.

Andersen, Christopher. *The Day Diana Died*. New York: William Morrow and Company, Inc., 1998.

Burchill, Julie. *Diana*. London: Weidenfeld & Nicolson Ltd., 1998.

Campbell, Lady Colin. *The Real Diana*. New York: St. Martin's Press, 1998.

Clehane, Diane. *Diana: The Secrets of Her Style*. New York: GT Publishing Corporation, 1998.

Diana, Princess of Wales, interviewed by Martin Bashir (transcript), *Panorama*, BBC Television, November 20, 1995.

Dimbleby, Jonathan. *The Prince of Wales: A Biography*. New York: William Morrow and Company, Inc., 1994.

"Diva of Style." *People* (March 1, 1996): 93–94

Donnelly, Peter. *Diana: A Tribute to the People's Princess*. Philadelphia: Courage Books, 1997.

Edwards, Anne. *Ever After: Diana and the Life She Led*. New York: St. Martin's Press, 2000.

Honeycombe, Gordon. *The Year of the Princess*. Boston: Little, Brown and Company, 1982.

Jephson, P.D. *Shadows of a Princess: An Intimate Account by Her Private Secretary*. New York: HarperCollins Publishers, Inc., 2000.

Krohn, Katherine. *Princess Diana*. Minneapolis: Lerner Publications Company, 1999.

Modlinger, Jackie. *Diana: Queen of Style*. Philadelphia: Courage Books, 1998.

Morton, Andrew. *Diana: Her New Life*. New York: Simon & Schuster, 1994.

——. *Diana: Her True Story—In Her Own Words* (Completely Revised Edition). New York: Simon & Schuster, 1997.

The Princess and the Press. Frontline. www.pbs.org/wgbh/pages/frontline/shows/royals/

Robertson, Mary. *The Diana I Knew: Loving Memories of the Friendship Between an American Mother and Her Son's Nanny Who Became the Princess of Wales*. New York: HarperCollins Publishers, Inc., 1998.

Seward, Ingrid. *Diana: An Intimate Portrait*. Chicago: Contemporary Books, Inc., 1988.

Simmons, Simone, with Susan Hill. *Diana: The Secret Years*. London: Michael O'Mara Books Ltd., 1998.

Smith, Sally Bedell. *Diana in Search of Herself: Portrait of a Troubled Princess*. New York: Times Books, 1999.

Spoto, Donald. *Diana: The Last Year*. New York: Harmony Books, 1997.

Index

Photo Credits